My Super duper Drawing activity book

This book belongs to :

....

You'll find the stickers at the back of the book!

I'm Doodle Monster. Look out for me inside!

priddy books

Monster Blobs

Turn these blobs into monsters.

Can you make me some buddies?

Vegetable Friends

Turn these vegetables into people!

Wooooh!

Doodle You

Doodle your reflection in the mirror!

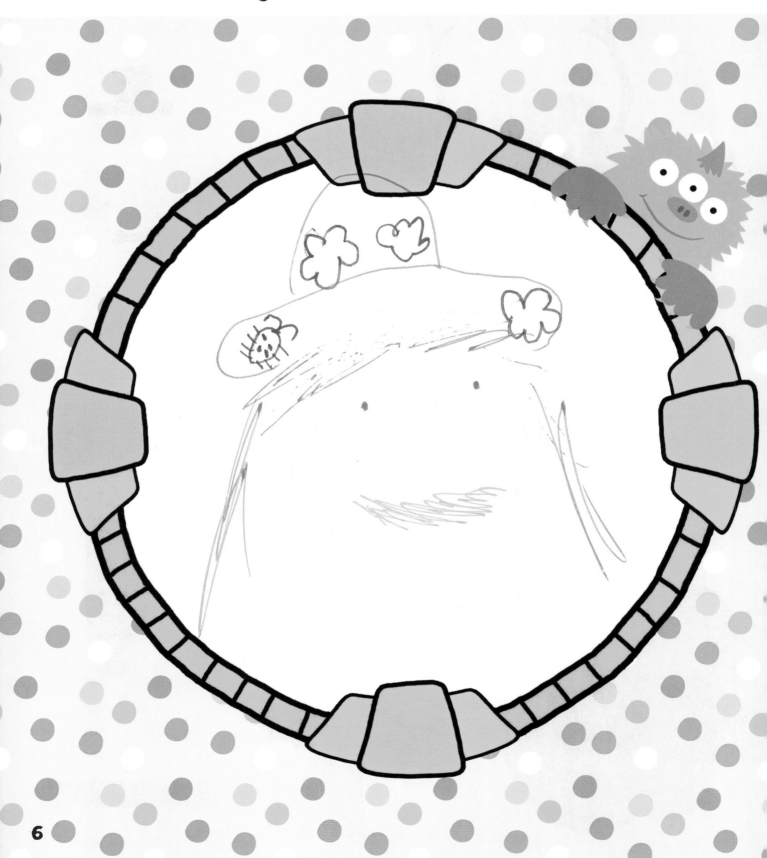

Pet Crazy

Draw two pets snuggling in this basket.

My Store

Fill the store with your favorite things.

what's your favorite fruit?

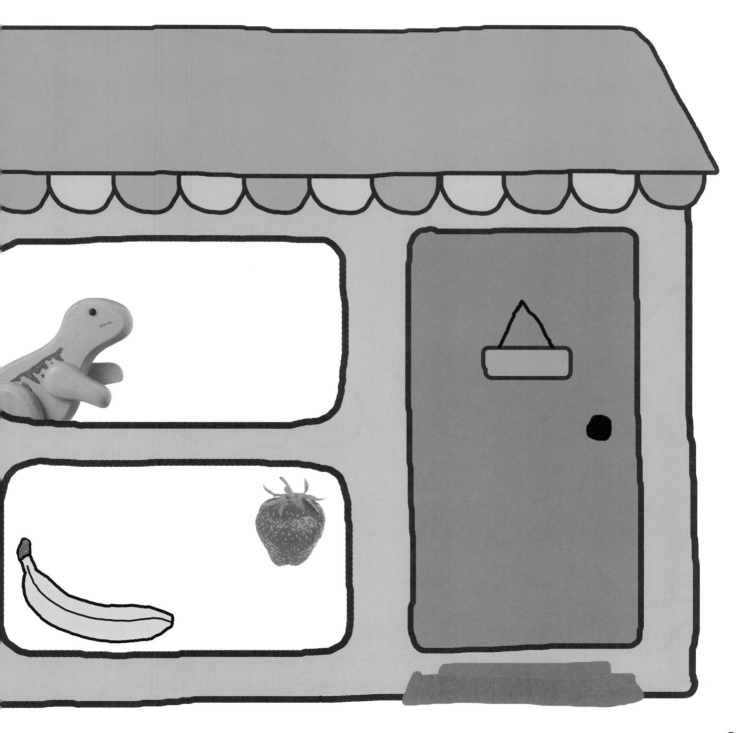

All Things Yellow

Use your yellow crayon to color everything in.

lemon

stars

chick

sun

banana

11

Old MacDonald's Farm

Find the animal stickers to fill Old MacDonald's farm.

what noises do the animals make?

Brrm, Big Rig

Who is driving this big rig? Doodle a grill on the front.

Star Pattern

Keep drawing around this star!

Fill the page with star power!

Button Buddies

These button buddies need more friends!

17

Which Way?

Add arrows all over this page!

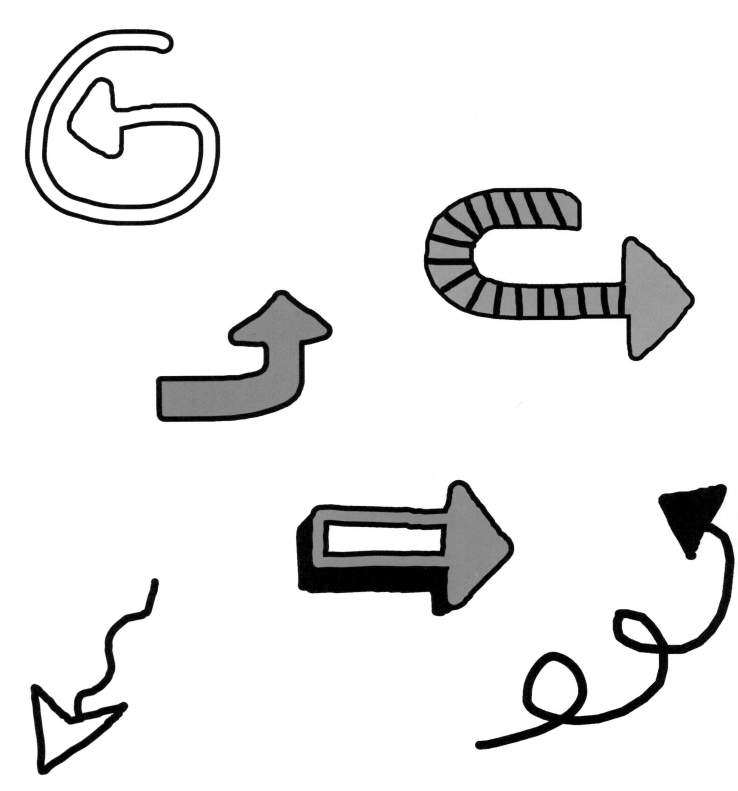

What's for Lunch?

Doodle your lunch in this lunch box!

Fingerprint Faces

Doodle happy faces onto these fingerprints.

I want a top hat!

Prehistoric Time

Color in these plants and fossils.

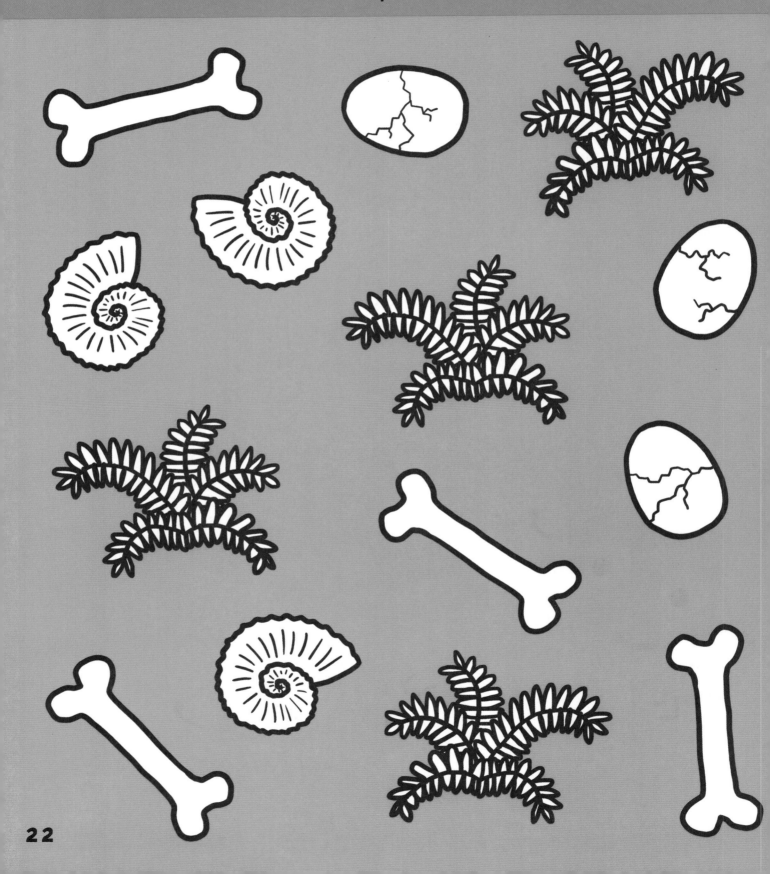

Pinocchio's Nose

Connect the dots to complete Pinocchio's nose!

1

5

2

3

4

Susie Stegosaurus

Can you find the stickers to give Susie her missing spikes?

In the Harbor

Find the stickers to add to the harbor scene.

Sweet Peas

Fill this page with sweet little peas!

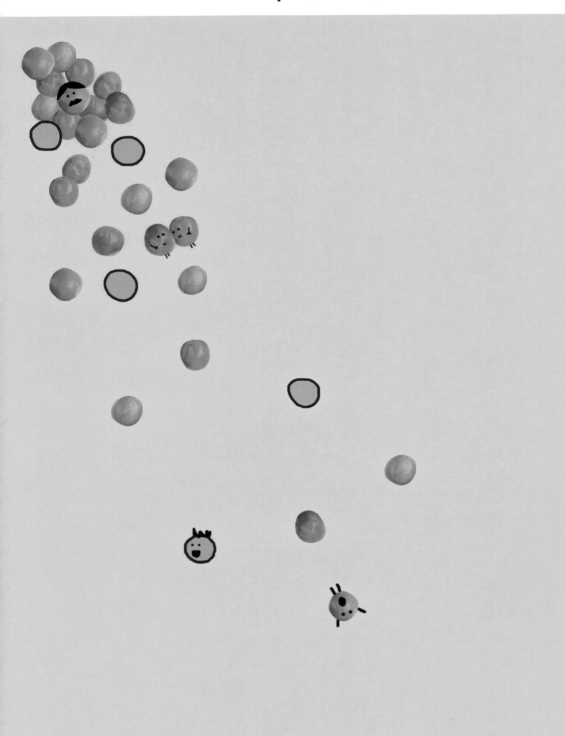

Farmyard Fun

who's in the barn? Doodle some more chicks!

Eggheads

28

Time for School

who is at school today? doodle in some students!

Backpack

Add patches and doodle designs!

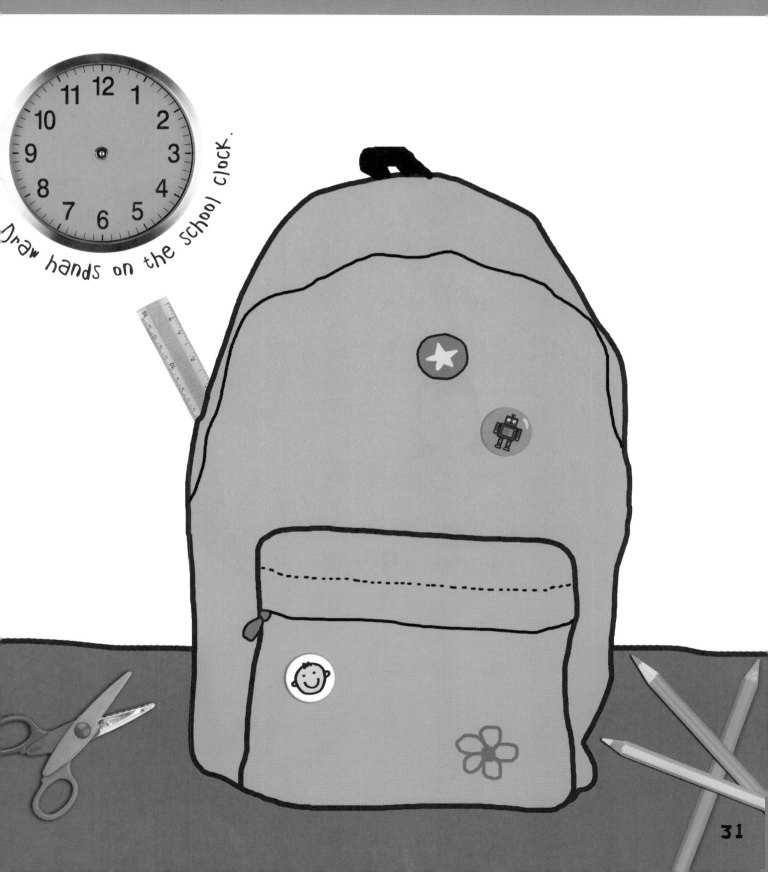

Draw hands on the school clock.

Superheroes

Turn these kids into superheroes.

What sort of superhero would you be?

Spider's Supper

How many flies can you count stuck in the web?

Learn to Draw

Can you copy this picture of a horse? Now color it in!

Harvest Time

Can you find the stickers to add to the farm and fields?

Where is the farmer?

Star People

where did everyone go?

Up and Away!

Doodle yourself on this passport.

Name: Cold Bobby

Age: 6

Birthday: June 15, 2011

I ♥ NY

SPAIN
04/10/2011

CANADA
06/02/2010

Sea Monsters

Turn these prints into sea creatures!

Monster Feet

Turn these feet into hairy monster feet!

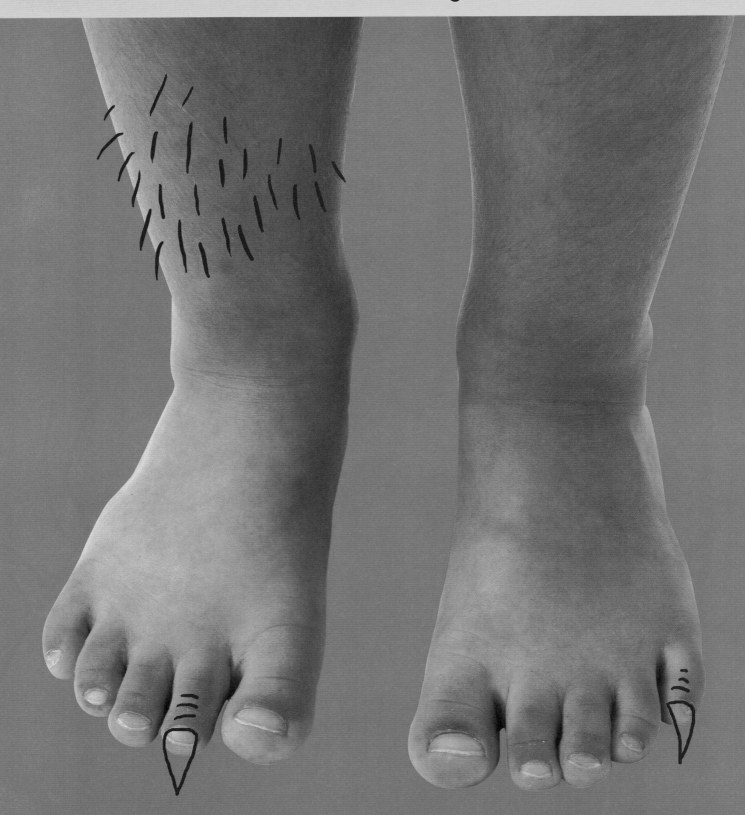

Fruit Float

Make these apples into underwater creatures!

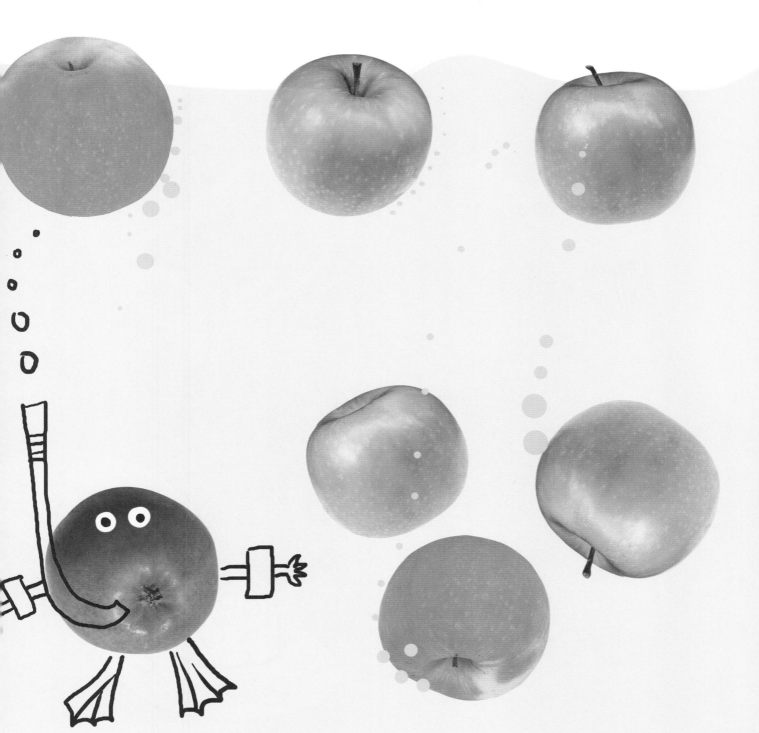

Rocket Power

Give this red rocket a fiery rocket trail!

Sweet Spiders

Turn the rest of these candies into spiders.

Doodle lots of legs!

Spooky Stall

Color in the horrible things for sale at the spooky stall.

Connect the Dots

Connect the dots to draw Sid the snail's shell.

Monkey Mischief

Color in these naughty monkeys.

Matching Mice

Can you draw a line between the matching mice?

Zebra Stripes
Turn these horses into zebras!

Up in the Air

Doodle a design on the balloon!

Lift, Lift, Lift

what is this crane lifting? Is it heavy or light?

Heart Doodle

Keep drawing around the heart.

Pencil Tops

54

Car Design

Design your dream car! What color will it be?

56

Funniest Doodle

Doodle your funniest-ever doodle in this frame!

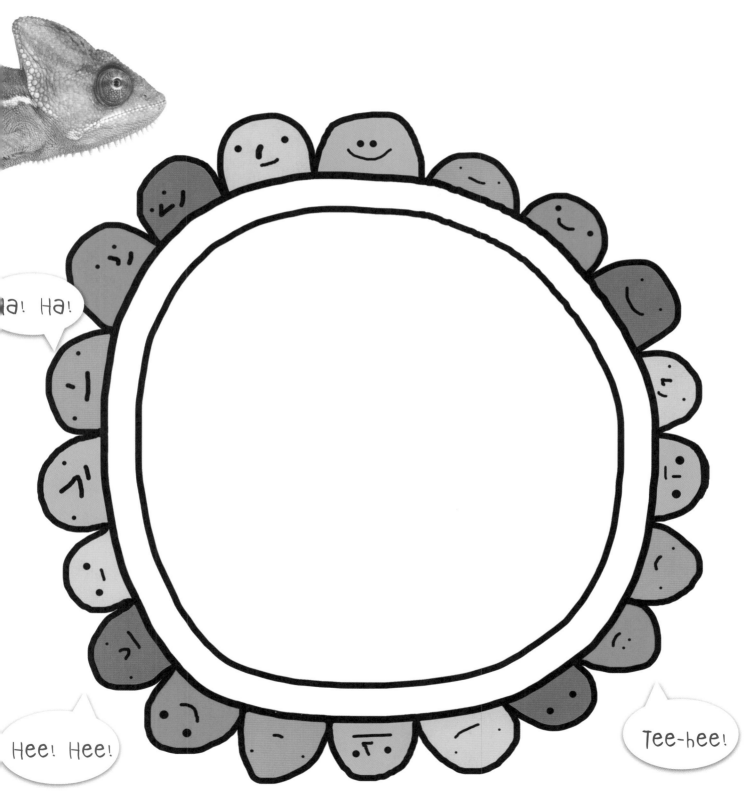

Sea Creatures

which sea creature has the most tentacles?

Learn to Draw

Can you copy this picture of a crane? Now color it in!

Builder's Yard

Park the truck stickers in the builder's yard.

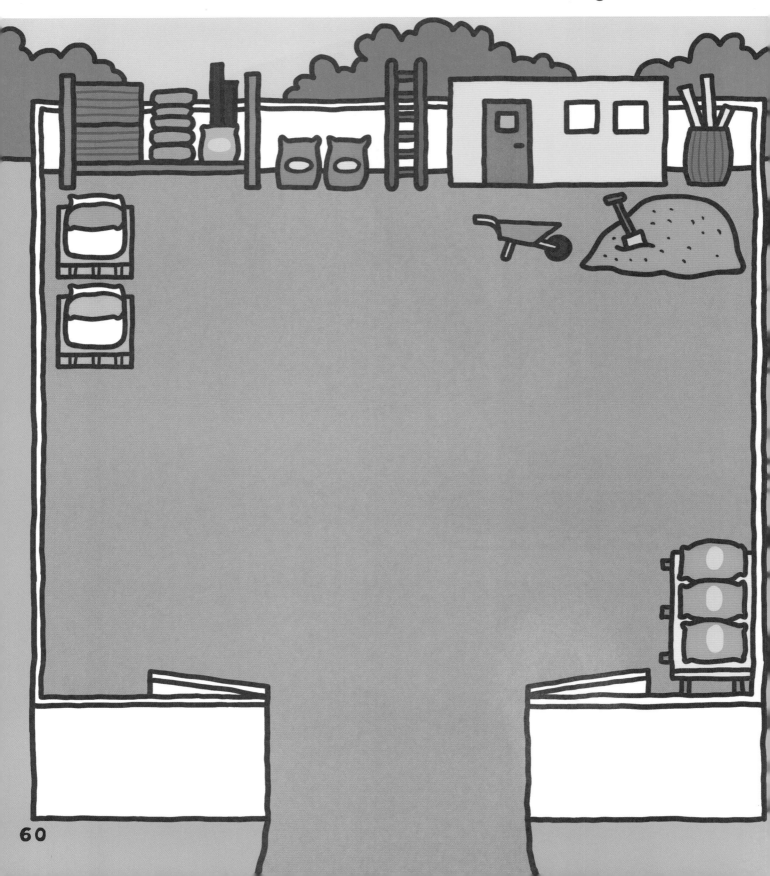

Love is in the Air

Decorate the sky with heart stickers.

Racetrack

draw some more cars on the racetrack!

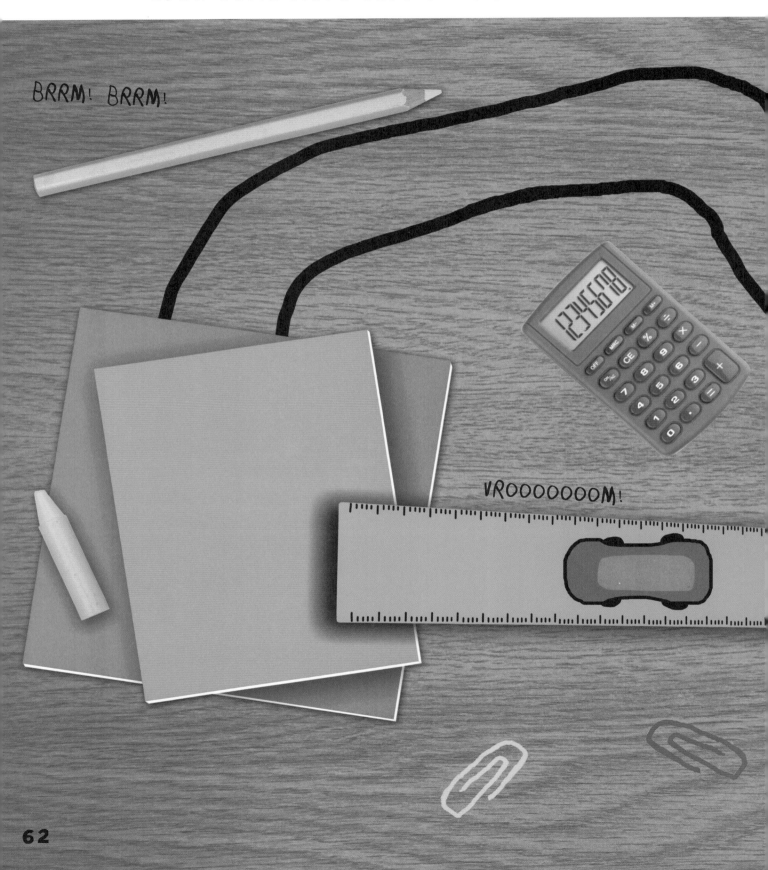

At the Art Gallery

what's on show at the art gallery?

Fill these frames with your best doodles.

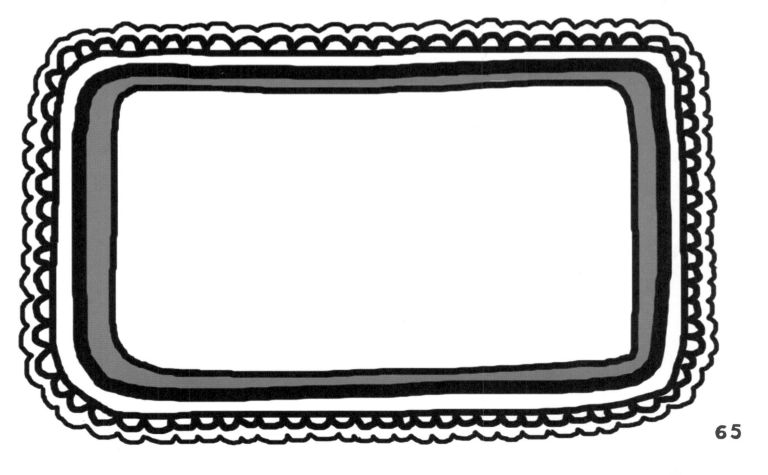

Wish Upon a Star

Doodle Monster and Doolila are looking at shooting stars.

Fill the sky with stars and doodle some sparkly trails.

Rubber Ducks

Doodle lots of patterns onto these cute rubber ducks.

69

Bunnies in the Barn

How many cute bunnies can you count in this barn?

Monkey Trail

Find the stickers, then help the hungry monkey find his snack.

Gingerbread House

Decorate the roof of the house with candy stickers.

Monsieur Cupcake

These cupcakes need faces and mustaches!

What is Doodle Monster drawing?

Splashing Around

Doodle some falling raindrops.

Birthday Cake

Add more layers to this cake!

T-shirt Design

Doodle your own cool design on my T-shirt.

Do you want to be a doodle fashion designer?

Candy Surprises

If you had a candy factory, what candies would you make?

In the Garden

can you make this fairy garden colorful?

Hammer Time

How many hammers can you count? Color in the tools.

Colorful Carriage

Color in this beautiful carriage.

Reindeer Sam

Poor Sam is missing an antler! Can you draw it for him?

Wanted

doodle yourself in this wild West Wanted poster!

Big Splash!

what are these kids jumping over?

Doodle, Doodle

Complete the doodle lines!

Candy Characters

Fill the jars with mischievous candy characters.

Nighttime Forest

Draw some spooky friends in the forest.

All Things Blue

use your blue crayons to color everything in.

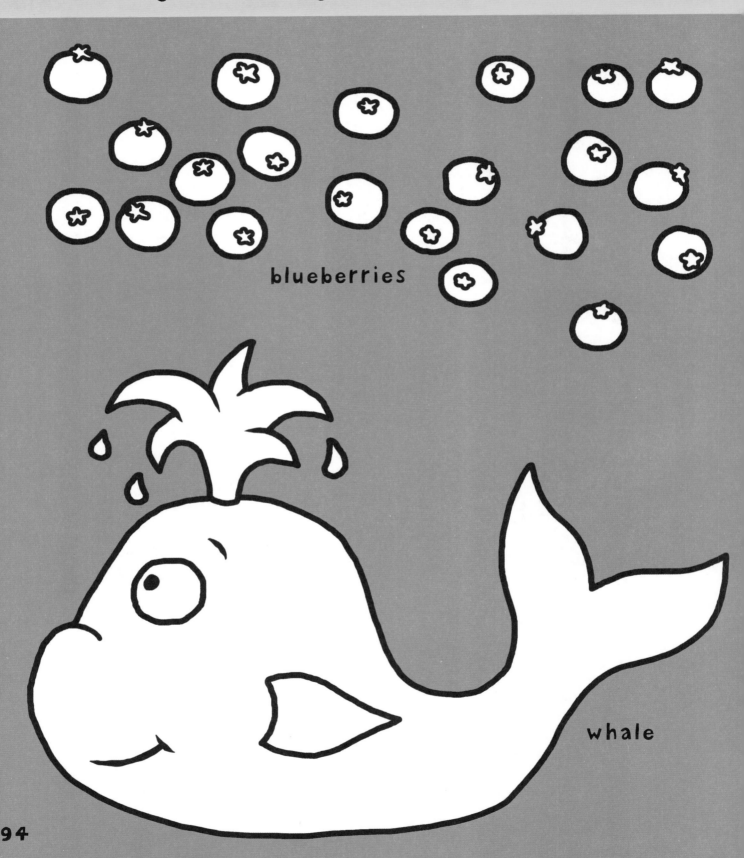

blueberries

whale

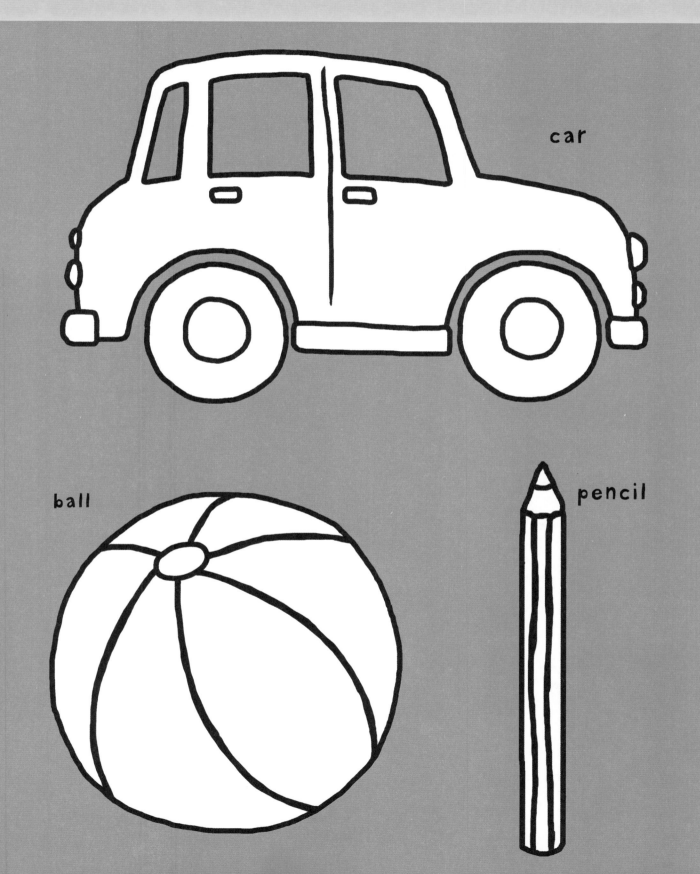

car

ball

pencil

Secret Cave

Find the stickers to decorate the pirate cave.

Shape Towers

Doodle lots of bricks to complete the towers!

Doodle the Opposite

This mouse is small. Draw something big!

How about
n elephant?

Balloon Party

who is holding these balloons?

Squares and Squares

Fill this page with black-and-white squares.

Patchwork

Complete this page by filling it with patches!

Bedtime

Make this room really messy!

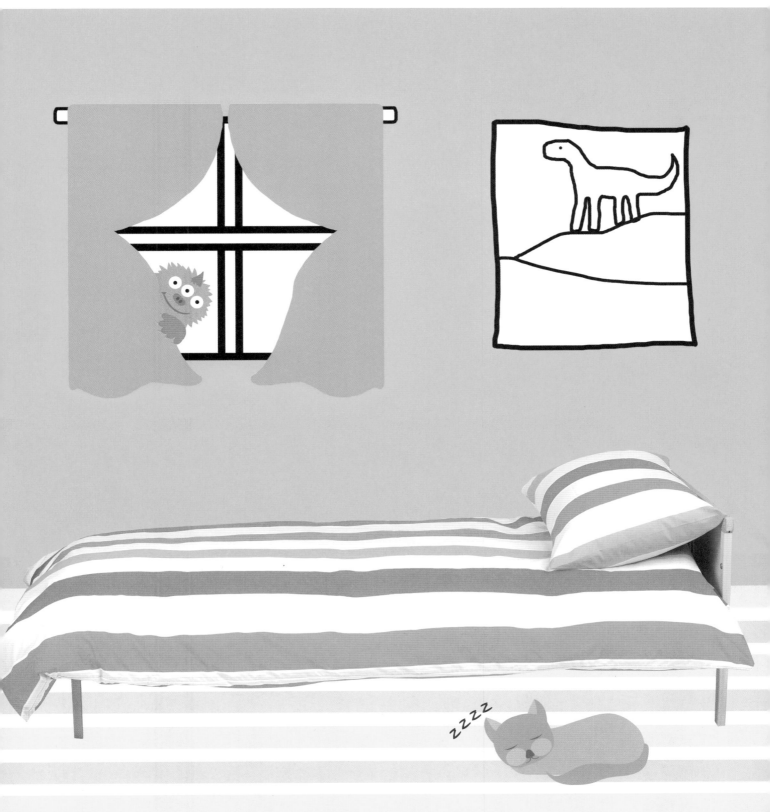

Showtime

Put on your own spectacular show!

Matching at Home

Can you draw a line between the matching objects?

Fishing Fun

Which gnome has caught the fish?

At the Stables

Can you find the stickers of the pretty ponies?

Dino Skeleton

Find the missing bone stickers to complete the picture.

109

Animals in Wigs

These animals like to change their hair.

Draw us some crazy hairstyles!

Odd Socks

These socks need patterns. Which sock is your favorite?

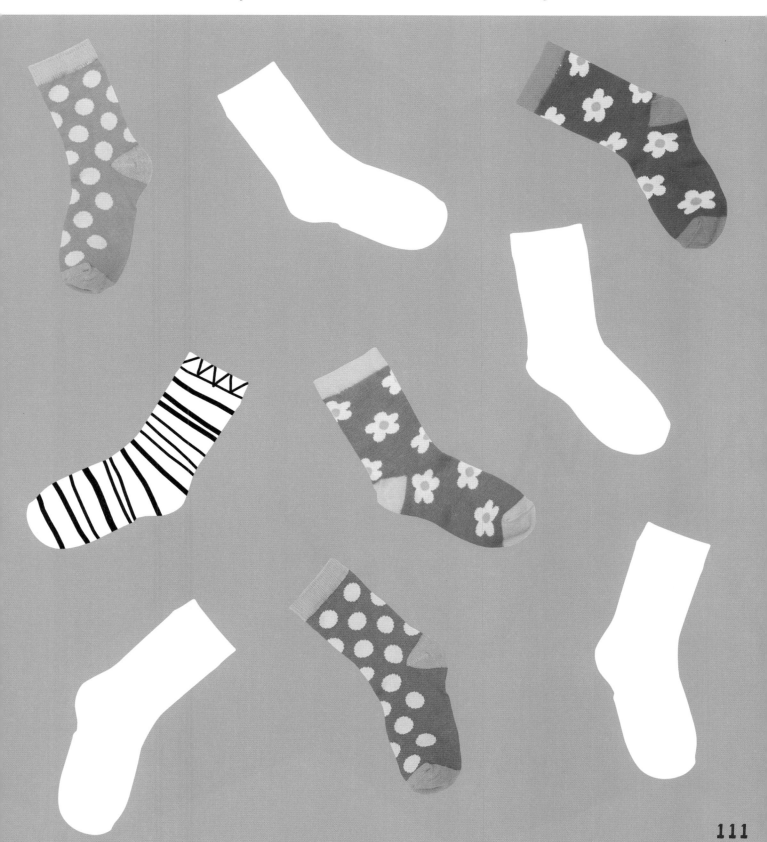

Zigs and Zags

Complete the zigzag lines!

Desk Pals

These pen friends are bored of staying still.

Give them all faces, arms, and legs.

Puppy Playtime

What are these puppies playing with?

WOOF!

Odd One Out

which is the scariest dinosaur?

Learn to Draw

Can you copy this picture of a cannon? Now color it in!

Fairy Kingdom

Find the stickers to decorate the fairy kingdom.

Can you find the fairy's frog friend?

Funny Faces

Give these faces hats, helmets, and sunglasses!

Fill the Shelves

Fill the shelves with your favorite toys.

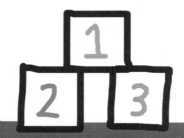

Cool Design

doodle your own design onto the sneaker.

Toy Box

Doodle your favorite toys in this toy box.

Robot Buddies

Turn these boxes into your very own robot friends!

Give them all names!

Chilly Penguins

which baby penguin has lost her wooly hat?

On the Moon

what color are the funny aliens?

Connect the Dots

Connect the dots to complete this lizard picture.

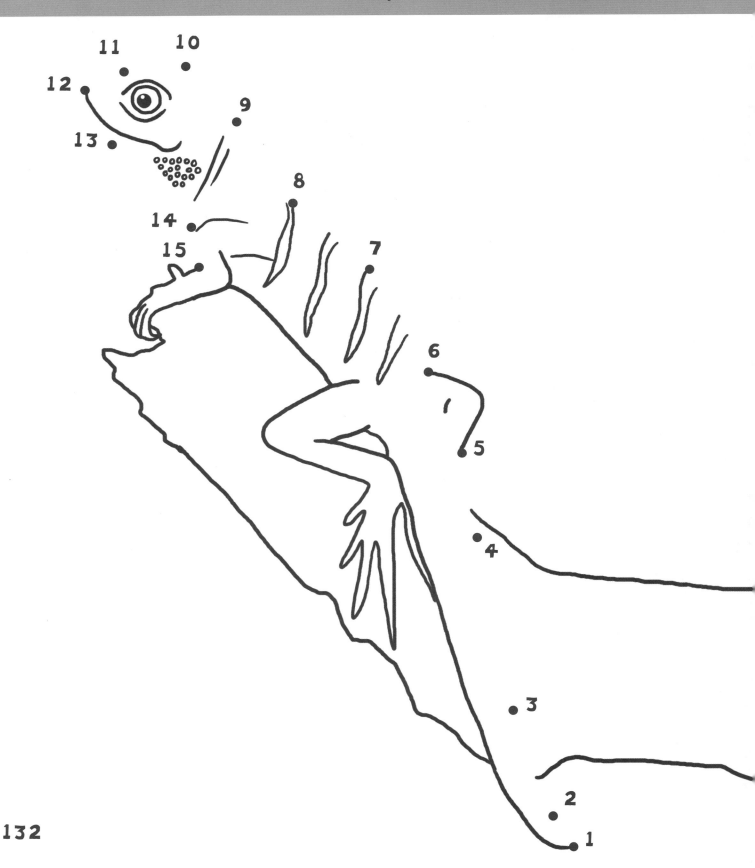

132

I Spy

Color in the pirate looking through the telescope.

Rain and Rainbows

Draw more raindrops and rainbows in the sky!

We love rain when it brings rainbows!

Scribble People

Turn these scribbles into people!

Little Monsters

Turn these everyday things into monsters.

Swirly Curls

Fill this page with swirls and curls.

Art Blobs

Turn these blobs into animals!

Counting Toads

Can you circle all of the toads?

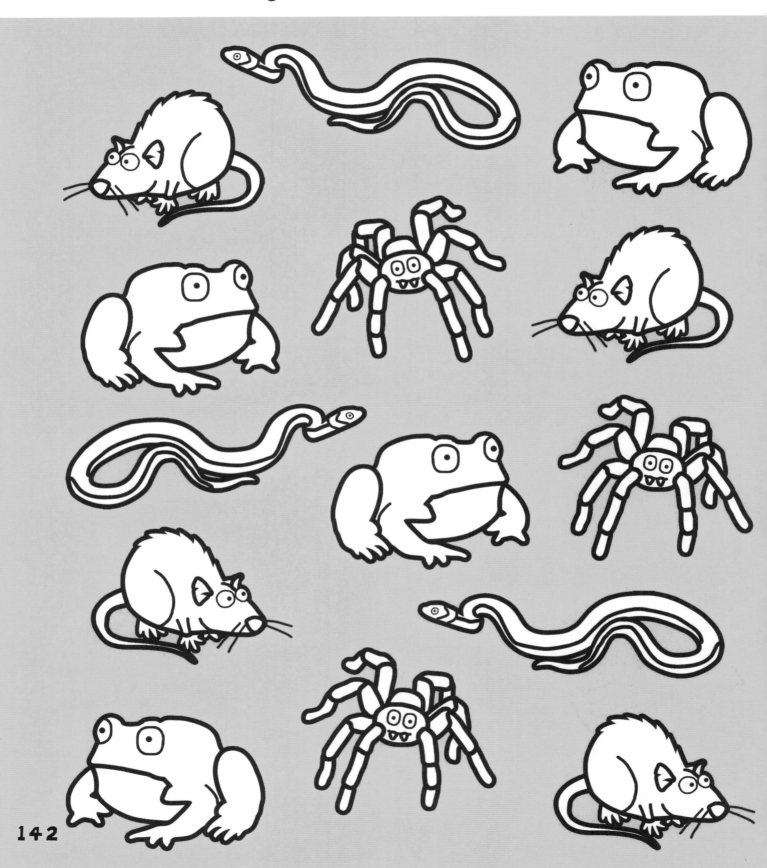

Food Fun

what color would you like the peas to be?

The Little Dog

Find the stickers to complete the dog's face.

144

Barry's Truck

Find the stickers to fill the builder's truck.

Nail Art

doodle some crazy patterns onto these nails!

Doodle some
bracelets
and rings!

Cool
nails!

Clothes Designer

Why not try some patterns you've done in this book?

Cardboard City

Turn these boxes into a super city!

Toast Family

Turn these pieces of toast into your family!

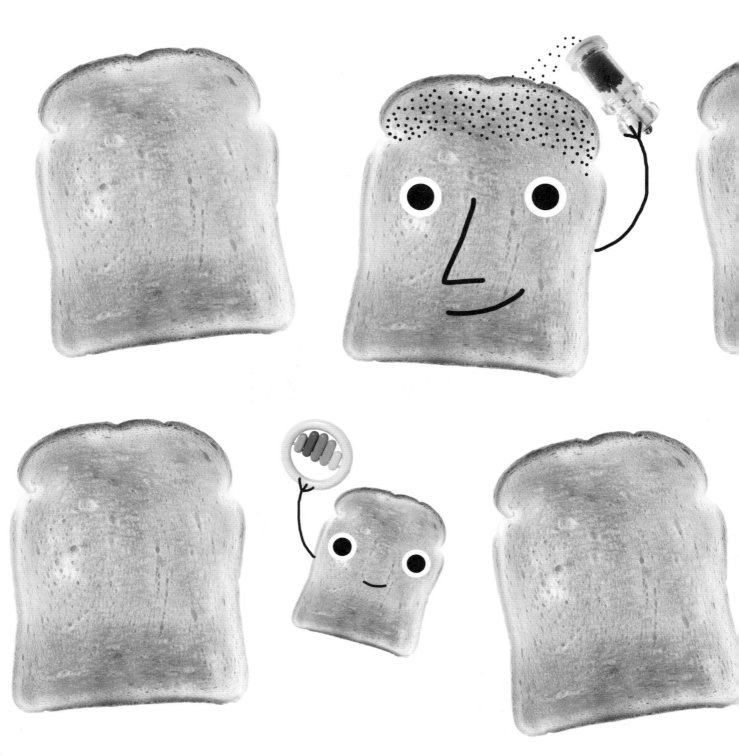

It's Your Garden

doodle things you find in your garden.

In Australia

Can you spot a baby kangaroo?

Matching Balls

Find the stickers, then draw lines between the matching balls.

What's in the Fridge?

Use your stickers to fill this fridge full of food.

Kids in Disguise

All these kids are super spies. Can you give them disguises?

who's that hiding behind the newspaper?

Fairy Wings

Turn these pencils into pretty fairies.

Give them all wings and faces.

Number Zoo

Turn these numbers into animals!

Treat Time

Decorate this ice cream with yummy sprinkles.

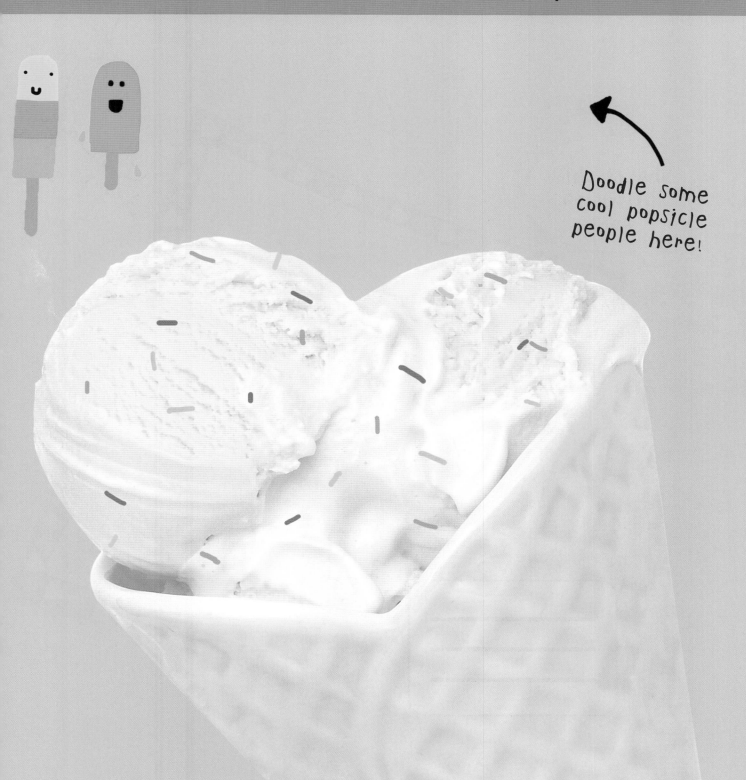

Doodle some cool popsicle people here!

Party Invitation

Doodle lots of pretty patterns onto this party invitation.

Lovely Bunch

Draw sweet little faces onto these grapes.

City Construction

Can you color in this picture of builders at work?

167

Odd One Out

Which one of the builders has lost his hard hat?

Princess Castle

Color in the castle hidden in the forest.

Do the Robot

These robots are missing parts of their robot bodies.

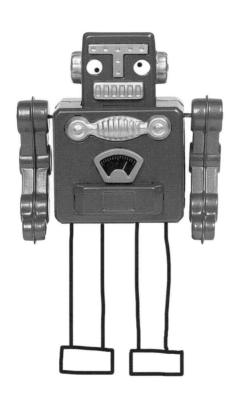

Fluttery Butterflies

Doodle pretty patterns onto these butterflies!

Fill this page with lots of triangles!

Turn these splats and splodges into anything you like!

Bookworm

Draw pictures from your favorite books onto the pages.

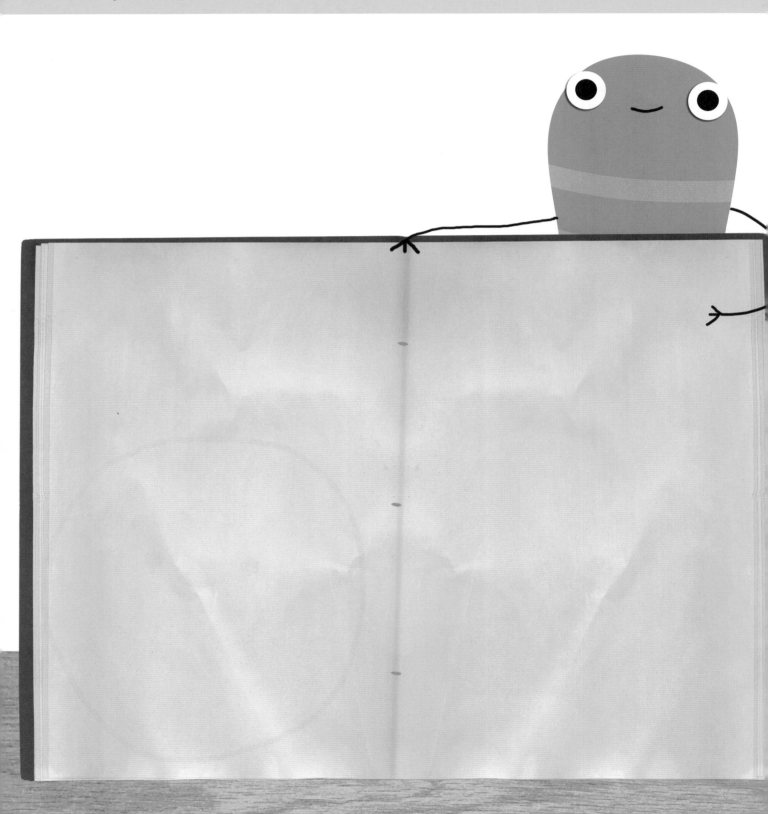

Super Sandwich

Make this sandwich the biggest one ever!

Hopping Around

which rabbit is the biggest?

Wicked Witches

Can you spot the five differences between these witches?

Prehistoric Land

Add your dinosaur stickers to this prehistoric scene.

Can you spot the dinosaur bone?

I Love . . .

doodle something that you love!

Yuckiest Doodle

Doodle a yucky, smelly doodle in the frame!

Feed the Pigeons

Doodle more pigeons and bread crumbs!

184

Top Secret

Doodle your secret ideas and designs!

Cookie Monsters

Turn these cookies into monsters.

Bats and Balls

Turn these colorful balls into bouncy bats!

Hairy Yaks

which yak is the hairiest?

Scary Maze

Help the children find the path to their house!

In the Sky

Find the stickers to complete this magical scene.

X Marks the Spot

Find the stickers to put on the map.

Paper Clip Pals

Turn these paper clips into people!

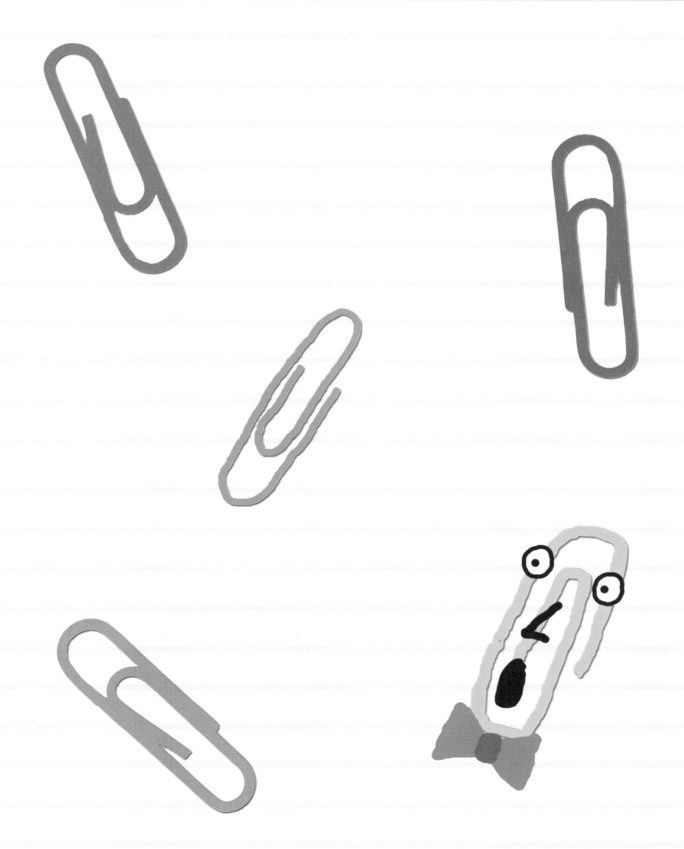

Let's Go!

who is on the Doodle Bus today?

196

Finish doodling patterns on the bus!

which things scare you?

Doodle them across these pages.

Prettiest Doodle

Draw your prettiest doodle in this frame!

My Hands

Make them furry like mine!

Grand Ball

Use your stickers to add guests to this beautiful ball.

Dino Trail

Find the stickers, then help Dino Dave find his way to Rex.

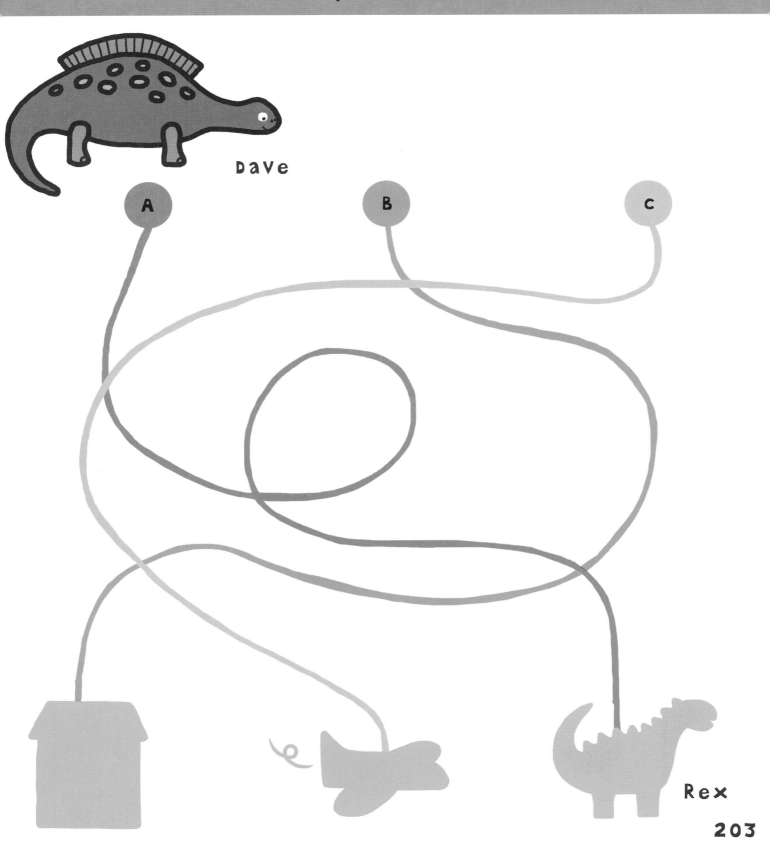

Dave

A   B   C

Rex

All Things Square

gift

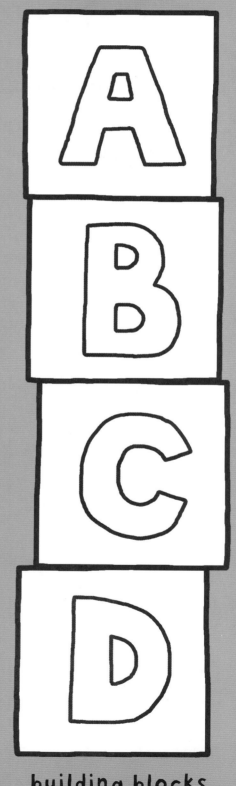

die

building blocks

window

Pineapple Party

Give these pineapples their spikes back.

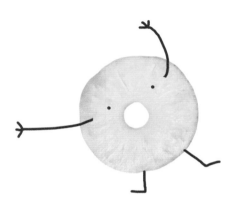

Doodle me a face!

Doodly Googly

Turn these googly eyes into crazy creatures!

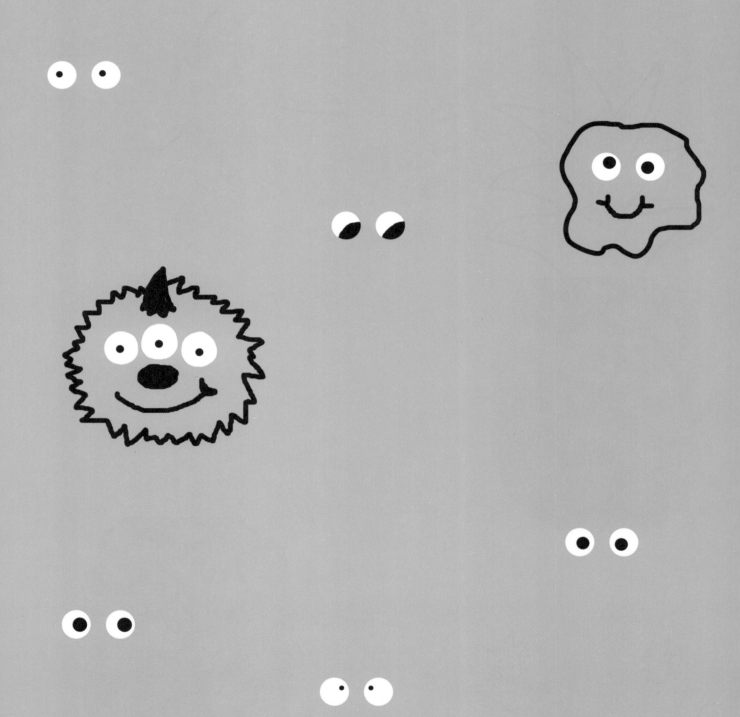

Ice Cream Parlor

Doodle more ice cream and toppings!

Meerkat Madness

what are these crazy meerkats doing?

Kite Flying

Can you make the kite really bright and colorful?

What's Missing?

which truck is missing its load?

Mermaid Lagoon

Can you find the sea creature stickers?

Now color in the palm tree!

CHOO! CHOO!

Flower Necklace

Can you give Sophie a pretty flower necklace?

The Pantry

The pantry is bare. Fill it with yummy food!

Crazy Invention

Help Doodle Monster complete his doodle machine!

222

Doodle, Doodle

Complete the doodle lines!

Learn to Draw

Copy this picture of a butterfly. Now color it in!

Bear Counting

How many panda bears can you count below?

Muddy Pigpen

Find the stickers to go in the pigpen.

who's playing in the mud?

Monster's Closet

what's in Doodle Monster's closet?

Leaf Creatures

Turn these leaves into friendly creatures!

Monster Madness

Fill the page with lots of mini monsters!

Hairy Monster

Doodle a face, arms, and more hair!

Give this monster a name!

236

Monster Boxes

Turn these boxes into squary little monsters!

Scary T. rex

Connect the dots to complete the T. rex, then color it in.

Turtle Maze

Guide Taylor the turtle through the maze to his friends.

start

Finish

239

Scary Trail

Help the prince get back to his castle.

Matching Grown-ups

Can you draw lines between the matching grown-ups?

Flower Doodle

Keep drawing around this happy flower!

Monster Races

Who will you put as the champion?

Tricky Patterns

Can you complete these tricky doodle patterns?

Gingerbread Friends

Finish off these gingerbread friends!

Alien Planet

Doodle your own alien planet.

what will you call your planet?

Pirate Saloon

How many green bottles can you count?

250

251

Palm Pirates

Can you find the coconut stickers to put on the tree?

Berry Bush

Add some berry stickers to the bush.

Candy Stripes

DRAW stripes on these candy canes.

Disco Doodle

Fill the page with swirls and musical notes.

Paint Splodge Zoo

Turn these paint splodges into animals.

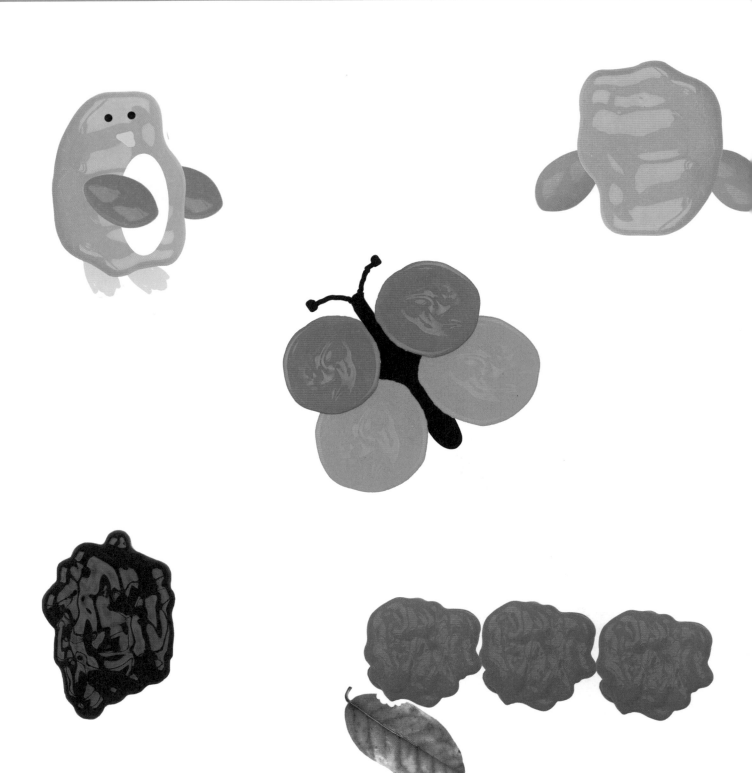

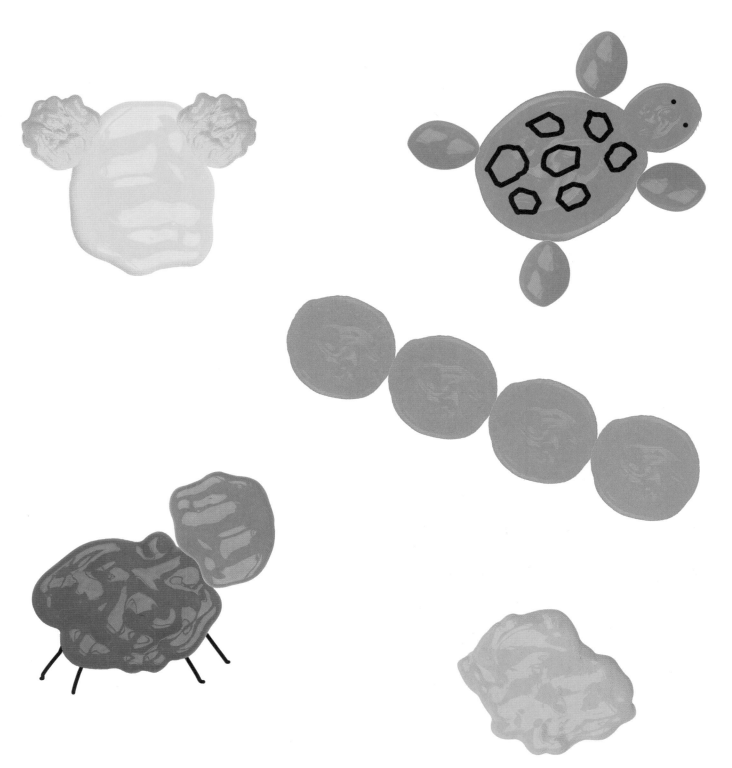

Royal Doodles

These stick friends are all princes and princesses.

259

Perfect Picnic

doodle all the yummy food you would eat at a picnic!

Postcard

doodle a really cool postcard design!

Friendly Lions

which lion is missing its tail?

Going to the Beach

Can you circle all of the sunglasses?

Dinosaur Face

Use your stickers to give this T. rex a scary face.

Fairy Castle

Can you find the flag stickers for this fairy castle?

Flamingo Beach

These pink birds need some legs.

Snail Trails

Doodle cool patterns onto these snail shells!

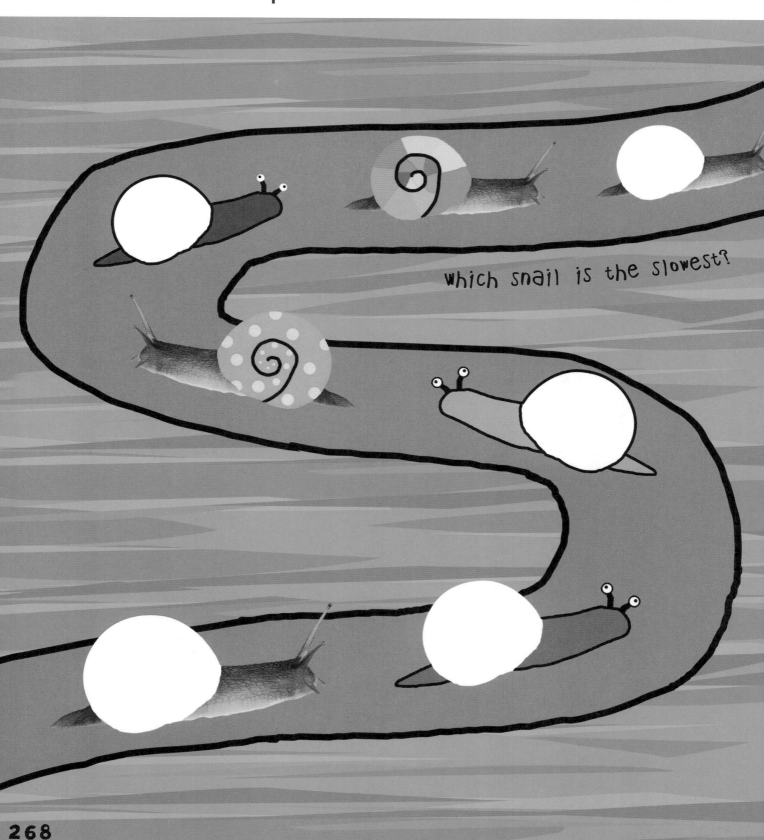

which snail is the slowest?

Square Doodle

Draw around the little square and fill the page!

New York, New York

who is in the city today?

Did you know New York is nicknamed the Big Apple?

Doodle Champ

Decorate these ribbons!

No.1
doodle

Champ

273

Picnic Maze

Follow the maze to help Princess Holly get to the picnic!

Scary Sharks

How many scary sharks can you count in this ocean scene?

Matching Friends

Can you draw a line between the matching dinosaurs?

Dinosaur Faces

Can you give Tommy Triceratops three horns?

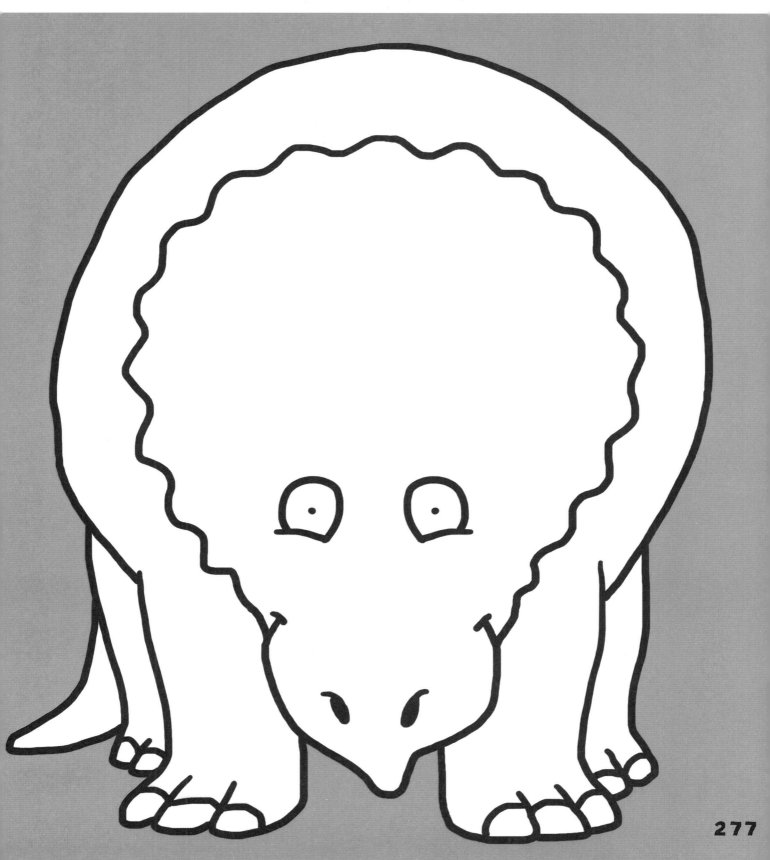

Roller Coaster Ride

Doodle the rest of this roller coaster!

Feathers

Doodle some more floating feathers around the page.

Creature Features

Turn these blobs into crazy, creepy creatures!

who has the scariest features?

Owl Family

draw the owl family hanging out in the treetops!

Top T-shirt

Can you design a new T-shirt for Emily?

Noisy Tractors

which tractor is Joe the sheepdog sitting in?

All Things Red

Use your red crayon to color everything in.

strawberry

heart

ladybug

flower

apple

fire truck

Fluffy Cat

Time for Tea

doodle pretty flowers onto this teapot!

Traffic Jam

Make this traffic scene really busy!

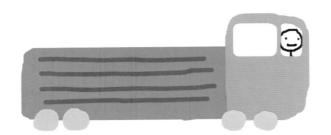

ONE WAY

My Town

Add windows, doors, and cars!

Monster Pets

Doodle some really freaky pets!

Make them bald or furry, fat or thin, ugly or cute!

Skull and Crossbones

Connect the dots to complete the picture.

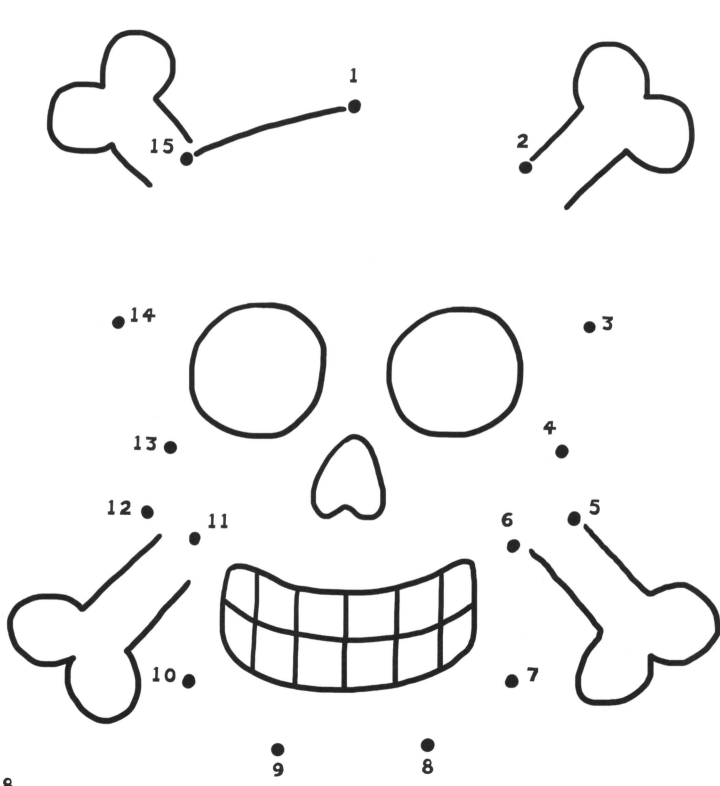

Colorful Castle

Can you color in the castle?

Toolbox Trail

Find the stickers, then help Trevor find his toolbox.

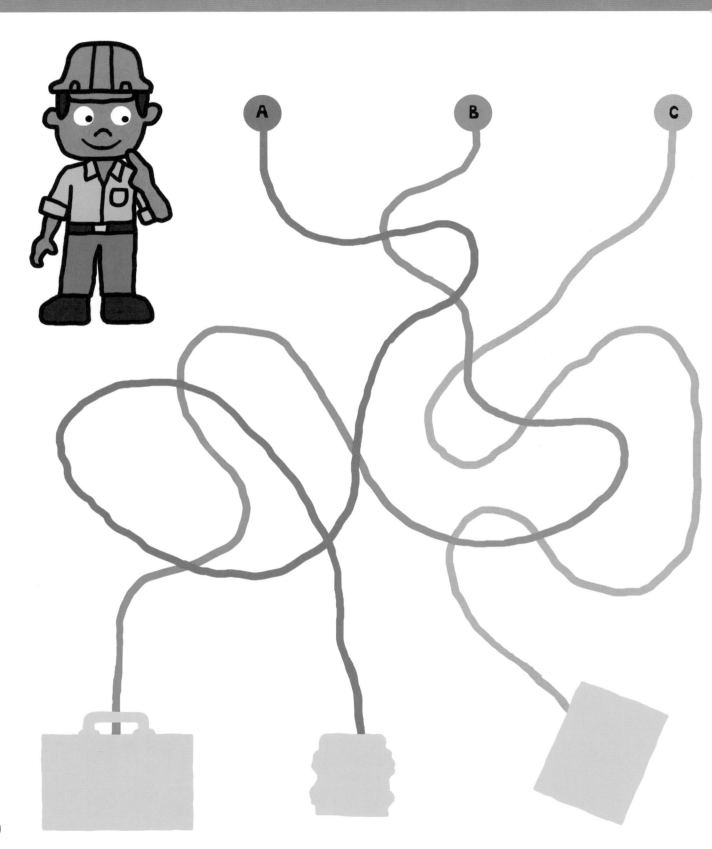

Page
12-13

Page
24

Page
25

Page
36-37

Page
60

Page 61

Page
73

Page
72

Page 96-97

Page 108

Page 109

Page 120-121

Page 144

Page 145

Page 156

Page 157

Page 180-181

Page 192

Page 193

Page 216-217

Page 202

Page 203

Page 253

Page 228-229

Page 252

Page 264

Page 265

Page 300